TO:

_____

*In all things God works
for the good of those who love him,
who have been called
according to his purpose.*

ROMANS 8:28 NIV

FROM:

_____

THE
PURPOSE
DRIVEN®
Life

SELECTED THOUGHTS AND SCRIPTURES

FOR THE GRADUATE

By RICK WARREN

inspirio™

Dear Graduate:

Congratulations! You have finally made it! The papers are finished, the tests have been taken, and you are now a graduate. You're closing the chapter on one part of your life and beginning to write a new one. You're excited and hopeful, scared and unsure, all at the same time. Perhaps you're asking, "Where do I go from here? What is my purpose in life?"

In this book, made especially for you, you'll discover that no matter who you are or where you live, God has five special purposes for your life. As you seek to fulfill them, everything else will fall into place.

God has great and wonderful plans for you. So, sit back, relax, and let him speak to your soul as you read. May God open your eyes so that you can see your unique purpose in this life.

—Rick Warren

WHAT ON EARTH AM I HERE FOR?

"Why do I exist?"
"Why am I here?"
"What is my purpose?"

These are the most fundamental questions you can ask in life. Have you ever asked these questions, wondering where to turn for the answer?

Contrary to what many popular books, movies, and seminars tell you, you won't discover your life's meaning by looking within yourself. You didn't create yourself, so there is no way you can tell yourself what you were created for! You must begin with God, your Creator. It is only in God that we discover our origin, our identity, our meaning, our purpose, our significance, and our destiny.

> *It is God who directs the lives of his creatures;*
> *everyone's life is in his power.*

JOB 12:10 TEV

It All Starts With God

The exciting truth is that God has never created anything without a purpose. Colossians 1:16 says: "For everything, absolutely everything, above and below, visible and invisible, ... everything got started in God and finds its purpose in him" (The Message). The very fact that you're alive means God has a purpose for your life!

> You know me inside and out, God,
> you know every bone in my body;
> You know exactly how I was made, bit by bit,
> how I was sculpted from nothing into something.

PSALM 139:15 THE MESSAGE

And you weren't created for just one purpose. You were created for five special reasons that are explained in God's Word. As you start this new chapter in your life, may you come to understand God's wonderful plan for you and find answers to life's most important questions.

> It's in Christ that we find out who we are and what we are living for. Long before we first heard of Christ and got our hopes up, he had his eye on us, had designs on us for glorious living, part of the overall purpose he is working out in everything and everyone.

EPHESIANS 1:11 THE MESSAGE

YOU WERE PLANNED FOR GOD'S PLEASURE!

*You, God, ... created everything
and it is for Your pleasure that they
exist and were created.*

REVELATION 4:11 NLT

The Bible says that God is love. It doesn't say God *has* love. It says God *is* love. Love is the essence of his character. God created you as an object of his love. You were made to be loved by God—that's your number one purpose.

Long before he laid down earth's foundations, God had us in mind, had settled on us as the focus of his love, to be made whole and holy by his love.

EPHESIANS 1:4 THE MESSAGE

Because of his love God had already decided that through Jesus Christ he would make us his children—this was his pleasure and purpose.

EPHESIANS 1:5 TEV

We know and rely on the love God has for us. God is love. Whoever lives in love lives in God, and God in him.

1 JOHN 4:16 NIV

he only accurate way to understand ourselves is by what God is and by what he does for us.

ROMANS 12:3 THE MESSAGE

No mere man has ever seen, heard or even imagined what wonderful things God has ready for those who love the Lord.

1 CORINTHIANS 2:9 LB

The LORD be exalted,
who delights in the well-being of his servant.

PSALM 35:27 NIV

As a father has compassion on his children,
so the LORD has compassion on those who fear him.

PSALM 103:13 NIV

God didn't *need* to love you. He wasn't lonely. He didn't need servants. He wasn't bored. God created humans because he wanted to love us. We were planned for his pleasure.

*The L*ORD *takes pleasure in his people.*

PSALM 149:4 NASB

God takes pleasure in those who honor Him;
in those who trust in His constant love.

PSALM 147:11 TEV

*The steps of the godly are directed by the L*ORD.
He delights in every detail of their lives.

PSALM 37:23 NLT

*The L*ORD *brought me out into a spacious place;*
he rescued me because he delighted in me.

PSALM 18:19 NIV

If the LORD *delights in a man's way,
he makes his steps firm.*

<small>PSALM 37:23 NIV</small>

*May the glory of the LORD endure forever;
may the LORD rejoice in his works.*

<small>PSALM 104:31 NIV</small>

*Smile on me, your servant, God;
Teach me the right way to live.*

<small>PSALM 119:135 THE MESSAGE</small>

*God's wisdom is something mysterious that goes deep into the interior of his
purposes. You don't find it lying around on the surface. It's not the latest
message, but more like the oldest—what God determined as the way to bring
out his best in us, long before we ever arrived on the scene.*

<small>1 CORINTHIANS 2:7 THE MESSAGE</small>

God made us in his image. That means that we are unlike anything else in all of creation. We alone were given the capacity to know God and to love him and to have him know and love us in return.

God created man in his own image, in the image of God he created him; male and female he created them.

GENESIS 1:27 NIV

The God who made the world and everything in it is the Lord of heaven and earth. ... And he is not served by human hands, as if he needed anything, because he himself gives all men life and breath and everything else. From one man he made every nation of men, that they should inhabit the whole earth; and he determined the times set for them and the exact places where they should live. God did this so that men would seek him and perhaps reach out for him and find him, though he is not far from each one of us. "For in him we live and move and have our being."

ACTS 17:24–28 NIV

I am your Creator.

You were in my care even before you were born.

ISAIAH 44:2 CEV

MADE TO LAST FOREVER

Right now, you're probably thinking only about your immediate future—college, your career, or maybe even marriage. And while those things are important, there is also another life waiting for you after this one. God designed you, in his image, to live for eternity.

> *God has ... planted eternity in the human heart.*
>
> ECCLESIASTES 3:11 NLT

> *When this tent we live in—our body here on earth—is torn down, God will have a house in heaven for us to live in, a home he himself has made, which will last forever.*
>
> 2 CORINTHIANS 5:1 TEV

> *I am here on earth for just a little while.*
>
> PSALM 119:19 TEV

> *This world is not our home; we are looking forward to our everlasting home in heaven.*
>
> HEBREWS 13:14 LB

This world is fading away, along with everything it craves. But if you do the will of God, you will live forever.

1 JOHN 2:17 NLT

We fix our eyes not on what is seen, but on what is unseen. For what is seen is temporary, but what is unseen is eternal.

2 CORINTHIANS 4:18 NIV

Every moment we spend in these earthly bodies is time spent away from our eternal home with Jesus.

2 CORINTHIANS 5:6 LB

If you call God your Father, live your time as temporary residents on earth.

1 PETER 1:17 GWT

Friends, this world is not your home, so don't make yourselves cozy in it. Don't indulge your ego at the expense of your soul.

1 PETER 2:11 THE MESSAGE

*T*here are many whose conduct shows they are really enemies of the cross of Christ. ... All they think about is this life here on earth. But we are citizens of heaven, where the Lord Jesus Christ lives.

PHILIPPIANS 3:18–20 NLT

The things we see now are here today, gone tomorrow. But the things we can't see now will last forever.

2 CORINTHIANS 4:18 THE MESSAGE

In God's eyes, the greatest heroes in this world are not those who achieve prosperity, success, and power in this life, but those who treat this life as a temporary assignment and serve faithfully, expecting their promised reward in eternity.

All these [heroes of the faith] died in faith. They did not get the things that God promised his people, but they saw them coming far in the future and were glad. They said they were like visitors and strangers on earth. ... They were waiting for a better country—a heavenly country. So God is not ashamed to be called their God, because he has prepared a city for them.

HEBREWS 11:13, 16 NCV

o the first purpose for your life is to know and to love God because that gives God pleasure.

The most important thing you can *know* in life is that God loves you.

"I have loved you with an everlasting love;
I have drawn you with loving-kindness," says the LORD.

JEREMIAH 31:3 NIV

You saw me before I was born, LORD,
and scheduled each day of my life
before I began to breathe. Every day
was recorded in your Book!

PSALM 139:16 LB

God decided to give us life through the word of truth so we might be the most
important of all the things he made.

JAMES 1:18 NCV

"I have carried you since you were born;
I have taken care of you from your birth.
Even when you are old, I will be the same.
Even when your hair has turned gray, I will take care of you.
I made you and will take care of you," says the LORD.

ISAIAH 46:3–4 NCV

he most important thing you can *do* in life is love him back.

Jesus said, "Love the Lord your God with all your heart and with all your soul and with all your mind. This is the first and greatest commandment."

<small>MATTHEW 22:37–38 NIV</small>

You are worthy, O Lord our God,
     to receive glory and honor and power.
For you created everything.

<small>REVELATION 4:11 NLT</small>

The LORD is pleased with those who worship him and trust his love.

<small>PSALM 147:11 CEV</small>

I will thank the Lord at all times.
     My mouth will always praise him.

<small>PSALM 34:1 GWT</small>

Take your everyday, ordinary life—your sleeping, eating, going-to-work, and walking-around life—and place it before God as an offering.

<small>ROMANS 12:1 THE MESSAGE</small>

God knows everything about you and he loves you. His deepest
desire is for you to know him and love him in return.

*"I don't want your sacrifice—I want your love. I don't want your offerings—
I want you to know me," says the Lord.*

HOSEA 6:6 LB

Figure out what will please Christ, and then do it.

EPHESIANS 5:10 THE MESSAGE

Jesus said, "If you love me, you will obey my commandments."

JOHN 14:15 TEV

*By Christ therefore let us offer the sacrifice of praise to God continually,
that is, the fruit of our lips giving thanks to his name.*

HEBREWS 13:15 KJV

*I will praise God's name in song
and glorify him with thanksgiving.
This will please the LORD.*

PSALM 69:30–31 NIV

So, instead of trying to do and say all the right things to make God love you, all you have to do is realize he loves you already, and love him back.

Well-formed love banishes fear. Since fear is crippling, a fearful life— fear of death, fear of judgment—is one not yet fully formed in love.

1 John 4:18 The Message

You, Lord, give perfect peace
    to those who keep their purpose
        firm
    and put their trust in you.

Isaiah 26:3 TEV

I am focusing all my energies on this one thing: Forgetting the past and looking forward to what lies ahead, I strain to reach the end of the race and receive the prize for which God, through Christ Jesus, is calling us up to heaven.

Philippians 3:13 NLT

Let's keep focused on that goal, those of us who want everything God has for us. If any of you have something else in mind, something less than total commitment, God will clear your blurred vision—you'll see it yet!

Philippians 3:15 The Message

God will even help you to know him more. All you need to do is ask, perhaps with a prayer like this:

"God, if I don't get anything else done today, help me to know you a little bit better and love you a little bit more. If, at the end of the day, I know you a little bit better and I love you a little bit more, I have not wasted this day. If I loved you and knew you a little bit more, I just fulfilled the first purpose of my life."

WHAT DRIVES YOUR LIFE?

❧

Perhaps you've been trying to find your purpose in life through a career, your education, or a relationship. These things alone, no matter how wonderful and fulfilling, are not your purpose. If you are searching for your purpose in life, don't worry about seeking out *your* gifts and talents, *your* goals or visions; start with your first and most important purpose—loving and knowing God. Everything else will fall into place when you seek first to fulfill this purpose for your life.

> *Jesus said, "Why do you worry about clothes? See how the lilies of the field grow. They do not labor or spin. Yet I tell you that not even Solomon in all his splendor was dressed like one of these. If that is how God clothes the grass of the field, which is here today and tomorrow is thrown into the fire, will he not much more clothe you? ...*
>
> *"So do not worry, saying, 'What shall we eat?' or 'What shall we drink?' or 'What shall we wear?' For ... your heavenly Father knows that you need them. But seek first his kingdom and his righteousness, and all these things will be given to you as well."*
>
> MATTHEW 6:28–33 NIV

What Makes God Smile?

hen you love God, you want to express it. That is called *Worship.* Whether you're singing a song or praying or simply enjoying a beautiful sunset and thanking God in your heart, that is worship.

God's pleasure is not in the strength of the horse,
    nor his delight in the legs of a man;
the LORD delights in those who fear him,
    who put their hope in his unfailing love.

Psalm 147:10–11 NIV

Come, let us bow down in worship,
    let us kneel before the LORD our Maker;
for he is our God
    and we are the people of his pasture,
    the flock under his care.

Psalm 95:6–7 NIV

Jesus said, "That's the kind of people the Father is out looking for: those who are simply and honestly themselves before him in their worship."

John 4:23 The Message

Worship is simply anything that gives God pleasure. And worship is the first purpose of your life!

Use your whole body as a tool to do what is right for the glory of God.

ROMANS 6:13 NLT

Jesus said, "As I have loved you, so you must love one another. By this all men will know that you are my disciples, if you love one another."

JOHN 13:34–35 NIV

May you always be filled with the fruit of your salvation—those good things that are produced in your life by Jesus Christ—for this will bring much glory and praise to God.

PHILIPPIANS 1:11 NLT

Offer your bodies as living sacrifices, holy and pleasing to God—this is your spiritual act of worship.

ROMANS 12:1 NIV

God has given gifts to each of you from his great variety of spiritual gifts. Manage them well so that God's generosity can flow through you. ... Are you called to help others? Do it with all the strength and energy that God supplies. Then God will be given glory.

1 PETER 4:10–11 NLT

As God's grace brings more and more people to Christ, ...
God will receive more and more glory.

2 CORINTHIANS 4:15 NLT

So whether you eat or drink or whatever you do, do it all for the glory of God.

1 CORINTHIANS 10:31 NIV

Whatever you do, work at it with all your heart, as working for the Lord, not for men.

COLOSSIANS 3:23 NIV

Just tell me what to do and I will do it, LORD.
As long as I live I'll wholeheartedly obey.

PSALM 119:33 LB

You were formed for a family!

God's unchanging plan has always been
to adopt us into his own family
by bringing us to himself
through Jesus Christ. And this
gave him great pleasure.

Ephesians 1:5 NLT

From the beginning of time, God has always wanted a family. He wants *you* to be a part of that family—a family that will last for all eternity.

Hebrews 2:11 is an amazing verse:

Jesus and the people He makes holy all belong to the same family. That's why He isn't ashamed to call them His brothers and sisters.

(NEW JERUSALEM BIBLE)

Jesus pointed to his disciples and said, "These are my mother and brothers. Anyone who does the will of my Father in heaven is my brother and sister and mother!"

MATTHEW 12:49–50 NLT

Jesus Christ calls us his brothers and sisters!

We're not just called to believe. We're called to belong—to belong to the family of God.

God is the One who made all things, and all things are for his glory.
He wanted to have many children to share his glory.

HEBREWS 2:10 NCV

See how very much our heavenly Father loves us, for he allows us to be called his children, and we really are!

1 JOHN 3:1 NLT

It was a happy day for God when he gave us our new lives, through the truth of his Word, and we became, as it were, the first children in his new family.

JAMES 1:18 LB

God has given us the privilege of being born again, so that we are now members of God's own family.

1 PETER 1:3 LB

You are all children of God through faith in Christ Jesus.

GALATIANS 3:26 NLT

The moment you were spiritually born into God's family, you were given some astounding birthday gifts: the family name, the family likeness, family privileges, family intimate access, and the family inheritance!

Since you are God's child, everything he has belongs to you.

GALATIANS 4:7 NLT

My God will meet all your needs according to his glorious riches in Christ Jesus.

PHILIPPIANS 4:19 NIV

I want you to realize what a rich and glorious inheritance God has given his people.

EPHESIANS 1:18 NLT

God has reserved a priceless inheritance for his children. It is kept in heaven for you, pure and undefiled, beyond the reach of change and decay.

1 PETER 1:4 NLT

So what does the family of God look like? Where can it be found?

God has given us the privilege of being born again so that now we are members of God's own family. That family is the church of the living God, the support and foundation of the truth.

1 PETER 1:3 NEW JERUSALEM BIBLE

When I think of the wisdom and scope of God's plan I fall down on my knees and pray to the Father of all the great family of God—some of them already in heaven and some down here on earth.

EPHESIANS 3:14–15 LB

Some of us are Jews, some are Gentiles, some are slaves, and some are free. But we have all been baptized into Christ's body by one Spirit, and we have all received the same Spirit.

1 CORINTHIANS 12:13 NLT

God's family is the church of the living God, the pillar and foundation of the truth.

1 TIMOTHY 3:15 GWT

What happens when a building has no support and foundation? It collapses. In just the same way, you need support from other people and a foundation to keep you strong in your walk with God. You find that loving support when you join your brothers and sisters in Christ's church—the family of God.

As you make your way in the "real world" it will be important to establish yourself on a solid foundation—surround yourself with Christian friends, mentors, and make attending church a priority. As a family, we all need each other!

In Christ the whole building is joined together and rises to become a holy temple in the Lord. And in him you too are being built together to become a dwelling in which God lives by his Spirit.

EPHESIANS 2:21–22 NIV

You are members of God's very own family, citizens of God's country, and you belong in God's household with every other Christian.

EPHESIANS 2:19 LB

Each part gets its meaning from the body as a whole, not the other way around. The body we're talking about is Christ's body of chosen people. Each of us finds our meaning and function as a part of his body. But as a chopped-off finger of cut-off toe we wouldn't amount to much, would we?

ROMANS 12:4–5 THE MESSAGE

The church is a *body*, not a *business*; a *family* not an *institution*. God says, "I formed you to be a part of my family."

We are the temple of the living God. As God has said: "I will live with them and walk among them, and I will be their God, and they will be my people."

2 CORINTHIANS 6:16 NIV

From Christ the whole body, joined and held together by every supporting ligament, grows and builds itself up in love, as each part does its work.

EPHESIANS 4:16 NIV

The way God designed our bodies is a model for understanding our lives together as a church: every part dependent on every other part.

1 CORINTHIANS 12:25 THE MESSAGE

When you become part of the family of God, you are so close that you are all actually part of the same body.

The body is a unit, though it is made up of many parts; and though all its parts are many, they form one body. For we were all baptized by one Spirit into one body—whether Jews or Greeks, slave or free—and we were all given the one Spirit to drink. Now the body is not made up of one part but of many. If the foot should say, "Because I am not a hand, I do not belong to the body," it would not for that reason cease to be part of the body. And if the ear should say, "Because I am not an eye, I do not belong to the body," it would not for that reason cease to be part of the body. If the whole body were an eye, where would the sense of hearing be? If the whole body were an ear, where would the sense of smell be? But in fact God has arranged the parts in the body, every one of them, just as he wanted them to be.

1 CORINTHIANS 12:12–18 NIV

Just as each of us has one body with many members, and these members do not all have the same function, so in Christ we who are many form one body, and each member belongs to all the others.

ROMANS 12:4–5 NIV

There should be no division in the body, but ... its parts should have equal concern for each other. If one part suffers, every part suffers with it; if one part is honored, every part rejoices with it. Now you are the body of Christ, and each one of you is a part of it.

1 CORINTHIANS 12:25–27 NIV

Not only do you need the body of Christ, the body of Christ needs you.

To one person the Spirit gives the ability to give wise advice; to another he gives the gift of special knowledge. The Spirit gives special faith to another, and to someone else he gives the power to heal the sick. He gives one person the power to perform miracles, and to another the ability to prophesy. He gives someone else the ability to know whether it is really the Spirit of God or another spirit that is speaking. Still another person is given the ability to speak in unknown languages, and another is given the ability to interpret what is being said. It is the one and only Holy Spirit who distributes these gifts. He alone decides which gift each person should have.

1 CORINTHIANS 12:8–11 NLT

God creates each of us by Christ Jesus to join him in the work he does, the good work he has gotten ready for us to do, work we had better be doing.

EPHESIANS 2:10 THE MESSAGE

The more you grow in your faith in God, the more you're going to love and treasure the church, because Jesus died for the church. Jesus loves the church (which includes all believers all over the world) so much, that the Bible compares it to a beloved bride.

Christ loved the church and gave himself up for her to make her holy, cleansing her by the washing with water through the word, and to present her to himself as a radiant church, without stain or wrinkle or any other blemish, but holy and blameless.

EPHESIANS 5:25–27 NIV

As a bridegroom rejoices over his bride, so will your God rejoice over you.

ISAIAH 62:5 NIV

Just like in an earthly family, where you receive love, but also give it, in God's family, we are called to love and care for our fellow members.

There are 58 "one anothers" in the Bible that teach us how to treat our brothers and sisters in the family of God.

They include:

LOVE ONE ANOTHER

Dear friends, since God so loved us, we also ought to love one another.

1 JOHN 4:11 NIV

Love means living the way God commanded us to live. As you have heard from the beginning, his command is this: Live a life of love.

2 JOHN 1:6 NCV

Show special love for God's people.

1 PETER 2:17 CEV

Jesus said, "Your strong love for each other will prove to the world that you are my disciples."

JOHN 13:35 LB

Encourage one another

Let us not give up meeting together, as some are in the habit of doing, but let us encourage one another.

Hebrews 10:25 NIV

Encourage one another daily ... so that none of you may be hardened by sin's deceitfulness.

Hebrews 3:13 NIV

If you know people who have wandered off from God's truth, don't write them off. Go after them. Get them back.

James 5:19 The Message

Pray for one another

Confess your sins to each other and pray for each other.

James 5:16 NIV

You should be like one big happy family full of sympathy toward each other, loving one another with tender hearts and humble minds.

1 Peter 3:8 LB

SERVE ONE ANOTHER

Serve one another in love.

GALATIANS 5:13 NIV

I want us to help each other with the faith we have. Your faith will help me, and my faith will help you.

ROMANS 1:12 NCV

As each part does its own special work, it helps the other parts grow, so that the whole body is healthy and growing and full of love.

EPHESIANS 4:16 NLT

Jesus laid down his life for us. And we ought to lay down our lives for our brothers.

1 JOHN 3:16 NIV

Whenever you possibly can, do good to those who need it. Never tell your neighbor to wait until tomorrow if you can help them now.

PROVERBS 3:27 TEV

When you participate in God's family, by loving and caring for each other, that's called *Fellowship*. Fellowship is the second purpose of your life.

If we walk in the light, as God is in the light, we have fellowship with one another, and the blood of Jesus, his Son, purifies us from all sin.

1 JOHN 1:7 NIV

Jesus said, "Where two or three have gathering together in My name, I am there in their midst."

MATTHEW 18:20 NASB

Real fellowship means being as committed to each other as we are to Jesus.

First John 3:16 says:

We understand what real love is when we realize that Christ gave His life for us. That means that we must give our lives for other believers.

(NEW JERUSALEM BIBLE)

Giving yourself, putting others first, isn't easy, but God asks you do it only because he did it first. He loves us, even though we aren't perfect, and his purpose for you is to do the same. Jesus wants you to love real people, not ideal people—because, after all, no one is ideal.

In real fellowship people experience authenticity and mutuality (the art of giving and receiving), sympathy, and mercy.

Love one another with mutual affection; outdo one another in showing honor.

ROMANS 12:10 NRSV

Make every effort to do what leads to peace and to mutual edification.

ROMANS 14:19 NIV

When people sin, you should forgive and comfort them, so they won't give up in despair.

2 CORINTHIANS 2:7 CEV

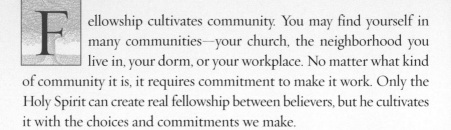

Fellowship cultivates community. You may find yourself in many communities—your church, the neighborhood you live in, your dorm, or your workplace. No matter what kind of community it is, it requires commitment to make it work. Only the Holy Spirit can create real fellowship between believers, but he cultivates it with the choices and commitments we make.

You can develop a healthy, robust community that lives right with God and enjoy its results only if you do the hard work of getting along with each other, treating each other with dignity and honor.

JAMES 3:18 THE MESSAGE

You are joined together with peace through the Spirit, so make every effort to continue together in this way.

EPHESIANS 4:3 NCV

Carry each other's burdens, and in this way you will fulfill the law of Christ.

GALATIANS 6:2 NIV

ultivating community takes honesty.

Speaking the truth in love, we will in all things grow up into him who is the Head, that is, Christ.

EPHESIANS 4:15 NIV

An honest answer is a true sign of friendship.

PROVERBS 24:26 TEV

Brothers and sisters, if someone in your group does something wrong, you who are spiritual should go to that person and gently make him right again.

GALATIANS 6:1–2 NCV

No more lies, no more pretense. Tell your neighbor the truth. In Christ's body we're all connected to each other, after all. When you lie to others, you end up lying to yourself.

EPHESIANS 4:25 THE MESSAGE

Cultivating community requires humility and courtesy toward one another.

Clothe yourselves with humility toward one another because God opposes the proud, but gives grace to the humble.

1 PETER 5:5 NIV

Live in harmony with each other. Don't try to act important, but enjoy the company of ordinary people. And don't think you know it all!

ROMANS 12:16 NLT

Give more honor to others than to yourselves. Do not be interested only in your own life, but be interested in the lives of others.

PHILIPPIANS 2:3–4 NCV

We must bear the "burden" of being considerate of the doubts and fears of others.

ROMANS 15:2 LB

God's people should be bighearted and courteous.

TITUS 3:2 THE MESSAGE

Be devoted to each other like a loving family. Excel in showing respect for each other.

ROMANS 12:10 GWT

Cultivating community takes confidentiality—avoid gossip at all costs. Community also takes frequency—you have to spend time together often to build great friendships.

Gossip is spread by wicked people;
they stir up trouble and break up friendships.

PROVERBS 16:28 TEV

Warn a divisive person once, and then warn him a second time. After that, have nothing to do with him.

TITUS 3:10 NIV

[The first Christians] worshiped together regularly at the Temple each day, met in small groups in homes for Communion, and shared their meals with great joy and thankfulness.

ACTS 2:46 LB

How wonderful it is, how pleasant,
for God's people to live together in harmony!

PSALM 133:1 TEV

You were formed for God's family and for regular, intimate, deep fellowship with other believers in Jesus.

Be kind and compassionate to one another, forgiving each other, just as in Christ God forgave you. Be imitators of God, therefore, as dearly loved children and live a life of love, just as Christ loved us and gave himself up for us as a fragrant offering and sacrifice to God.

Ephesians 4:32—5:2 NIV

Let the peace of Christ rule in your hearts, since as members of one body you were called to peace.

Colossians 3:15 NIV

If one part of the body suffers, all the other parts suffer with it. Or if one part of our body is honored, all the other parts share its honor.

1 Corinthians 12:26 NCV

Jesus said, "Your love for one another will prove to the world that you are my disciples."

John 13:35 NLT

God deeply desires that we experience oneness and harmony with each other. If you've ever been a part of a team, whether it be a sports team or a project team at work or school, you know that all the members must work toward the same goal or nothing gets done. Unity is the soul of fellowship.

Work hard at living at peace with others.

1 PETER 3:11 NLT

Do everything possible on your part to live in peace with everybody.

ROMANS 12:18 TEV

Let there be real harmony so there won't be divisions in the church. I plead with you to be of one mind united in thought and purpose.

1 CORINTHIANS 1:10 NLT

Let us concentrate on the things which make for harmony, and on the growth of one another's character.

ROMANS 14:19 PH.

You're blessed when you can show people how to cooperate instead of compete or fight. That's when you discover who you really are, and your place in God's family.

MATTHEW 5:9 THE MESSAGE

ost of all, let love guide your life, for then the whole church will stay together in perfect harmony.

COLOSSIANS 3:14 LB

Jesus said, "Blessed are the peacemakers,
    for they will be called sons of God."

MATTHEW 5:9 NIV

Fellowship, being adopted as a part of God's family, is the second great purpose for your life.

We proclaim to you what we have seen and heard, [about Jesus] so that you also may have fellowship with us. And our fellowship is with the Father and with his Son, Jesus Christ.

1 JOHN 1:3 NIV

Jesus came and preached peace to you who were far away and peace to those who were near. For through him we both have access to the Father by one Spirit. Consequently, you are no longer foreigners and aliens, but fellow citizens with God's people and members of God's household, built on the foundation of the apostles and prophets, with Christ Jesus himself as the chief cornerstone.

EPHESIANS 2:17–20 NIV

Jesus prayed, "My prayer is not for [my disciples] alone. I pray also for those who will believe in me through their message, that all of them may be one, Father, just as you are in me and I am in you. May they also be in us so that the world may believe that you have sent me."

JOHN 17:20–21 NIV

You Were Created to Become Like Christ!

From the very beginning God decided
that those who came to him—and all
along he knew who would—should
become like his Son, so his Son would be
the First, with many brothers.

ROMANS 8:29 LB

The third reason God created you was to become like his Son, Jesus. This has been God's plan from the beginning of time. In Genesis 1:26, God says, "Let us make man in our image." At the dawn of the world, God planned for you to have the character of Christ—to be godly.

You were ... created to be like God,
truly righteous and holy.

EPHESIANS 4:24 GWT

God has saved us and called us to a holy life—not because of anything we have done but because of his own purpose and grace. This grace was given us in Christ Jesus before the beginning of time.

2 TIMOTHY 1:9 NIV

We look at this Son and see God's original purpose in everything created.

COLOSSIANS 1:15 THE MESSAGE

We were made with the very breath of God.

The LORD God formed the man from the dust of the ground and breathed into his nostrils the breath of life, and the man became a living being.

GENESIS 2:7 NIV

Because you were created to be like Christ, God is more interested in what you *are* than in what you *do*. You're not taking your diplomas or earnings or awards into heaven, but you are taking your *character*.

> *Jesus said, "Do not store up for yourselves treasures on earth, where moth and rust destroy, and where thieves break in and steal. But store up for yourselves treasures in heaven, where moth and rust do not destroy, and where thieves do not break in and steal. For where your treasure is, there your heart will be also."*
>
> MATTHEW 6:19–21 NIV

Take on an entirely new way of life—
a God-fashioned life, a life renewed from the inside
and working itself into your conduct as
God accurately reproduces his character in you.

EPHESIANS 4:22 THE MESSAGE

> *In keeping with God's promise we are looking forward to a new heaven and a new earth, the home of righteousness. So then, dear friends, since you are looking forward to this, make every effort to be found spotless, blameless and at peace with him.*
>
> 2 PETER 3:13–14 NIV

I f God wants to make us like Jesus, the question becomes, *"What is Jesus like?"*

If you want a perfect picture of Jesus you can find it in Galatians 5:22–23:

The fruit of the Spirit is love, joy, peace, patience, kindness, goodness, faithfulness, gentleness and self-control. (NIV)

Those nine qualities are a picture of Jesus, and so God wants to build those nine qualities into your life.

Make every effort to add to your faith goodness; and to goodness, knowledge; and to knowledge, self-control; and to self-control, perseverance; and to perseverance, godliness; and to godliness, brotherly kindness; and to brotherly kindness, love.

2 PETER 1:5–7 NIV

As the Spirit of the Lord works within us, we become more and more like him and reflect his glory even more.

2 CORINTHIANS 3:18 NLT

God is working in you, giving you the desire to obey him and the power to do what pleases him.

PHILIPPIANS 2:13 NLT

So how does God do it? How do we become like Jesus? Do I just walk down the street one day and ... zap! I'm full of love! Do I go to a conference or read a book or listen to a tape and ... bang! I'm filled with patience!

No. God does not zap. There's no such thing as instant spiritual maturity. So how does God make me like Christ?

God makes you like Jesus by putting you in the situations that are completely contrary to the qualities he wants you to develop.

LOVE

It's easy to love *lovely* people. God teaches you real love by putting you around some *unlovely* people.

> *The LORD has anointed me*
> *to preach good news to the poor.*
> *He has sent me to bind up the brokenhearted,*
> *to proclaim freedom for the captives*
> *and release from darkness for the prisoners.*

ISAIAH 61:1 NIV

JOY

❧

Joy is different than happiness. Happiness depends on circumstances. I go to Disneyland I'm happy. I go home and realize how much I spent, I'm not happy. Joy is internal. Happiness is external. God will teach you real joy in the middle of grief.

Rejoice that you participate in the sufferings of Christ, so that you may be overjoyed when his glory is revealed. If you are insulted because of the name of Christ, you are blessed, for the Spirit of glory and of God rests on you.

1 Peter 4:13–14 NIV

Our light and momentary troubles are achieving for us an eternal glory that far outweighs them all.

2 Corinthians 4:17 NIV

Jesus said, "In this world you will have trouble. But take heart! I have overcome the world."

John 16:33 NIV

PEACE

Where do you learn peace? Out fishing on a beautiful stream? Anybody can be peaceful in that kind of environment. So instead, God will put you in traffic jams. He'll give you a day when you have a pop quiz and a rush project and your friend wants to borrow money that you don't have and your computer crashes and your car breaks down and everything's going wrong. And it is there, in the middle of the storm, that you learn peace.

"When you pass through the waters,
    I will be with you;
and when you pass through the rivers,
    they will not sweep over you.
When you walk through the fire,
    you will not be burned;
the flames will not set you ablaze," says the Lord.

Isaiah 43:2 NIV

We know that God causes everything to work together for the good of those who love God and are called according to his purpose for them. For God knew his people in advance, and he chose them to become like his Son.

Romans 8:28–29 NLT

PATIENCE

od's plan for teaching us patience is pretty obvious. He'll put you in doctor's offices and long lines at the DMV.

There was a time in my life when I said, "O God! I need patience" and instead of my struggles getting better they got worse. Finally, after about six months I realized I was a lot more patient than when I started. God was giving me the patience I asked for through those situations.

We ... rejoice in our sufferings, because we know that suffering produces perseverance; perseverance, character; and character, hope.

ROMANS 5:3–4 NIV

Don't try to get out of anything prematurely. Let it do its work so you become mature and well-developed.

JAMES 1:4 THE MESSAGE

"These things I plan won't happen right away. Slowly, steadily, surely, the time approaches when the vision will be fulfilled. If it seems slow, do not despair, for these things will surely come to pass. Just be patient! They will not be overdue a single day!" says the Lord.

HABAKKUK 2:3 LB

Once you understand your purpose is to be like Christ, life begins to make more sense. When difficult, unexplainable things happen, we begin to understand why—to make us like Jesus Christ!

As God works in you to make you like his Son, he is going to take you through the struggles Jesus experienced.

Were there times when Jesus was lonely?

Yes.

Were there times when Jesus was tired?

Yes.

Were there times when he was misunderstood and criticized unjustly?

Yes.

Did God take care of and strengthen Jesus through it all?

Yes. And he'll do the same for you.

In your lives you must think and act like Christ Jesus.

PHILIPPIANS 2:5 NCV

No matter how difficult the situation, you can learn from it if you will respond to it with the question, "What does Jesus want me to learn?"

While effort has nothing to do with your salvation, it has much to do with your spiritual growth. We must cooperate with the Holy Spirit's work in our lives. At least eight times in the New Testament we are told to "make every effort" in our growth toward becoming like Jesus.

> *Jesus said, "Make every effort to enter through the narrow door [to follow Christ], because many, I tell you, will try to enter and will not be able to."*
>
> LUKE 13:24 NIV

Make every effort to give yourself to God as the kind of person he will accept. Be a worker who is not ashamed and who uses the true teaching in the right way.

2 TIMOTHY 2:15 NCV

> *Make every effort to live in peace with all men and to be holy; without holiness no one will see the Lord.*
>
> HEBREWS 12:14 NIV

W e have three responsibilities in becoming like Christ.

First, we must choose to let go of old ways of acting.

Everything—and I do mean everything—connected with that old way of life has to go. It's rotten through and through. Get rid of it!

EPHESIANS 4:22 THE MESSAGE

Second, we must change the way we think.

Let the Spirit change your way of thinking.

EPHESIANS 4:23 CEV

Third, we must "put on" the character of Christ by developing new, godly habits.

Put on the new self, created to be like God in true righteousness and holiness.

EPHESIANS 4:24 NIV

As you come to Christ, the living Stone—rejected by men but chosen by God and precious to him—you also, like living stones, are being built into a spiritual house to be a holy priesthood, offering spiritual sacrifices acceptable to God through Jesus Christ. For in Scripture it says:

> "See, I lay a stone in Zion,
> a chosen and precious cornerstone,
> and the one who trusts in him
> will never be put to shame."

1 Peter 2:4–6 NIV

God's third purpose for your life, the process that God uses to make you like Jesus, is called *Discipleship*. God wants you to become a mature member of his family, just as Christ is.

I want to know Christ and the power of his resurrection and the fellowship of sharing in his sufferings, becoming like him in his death, and so, somehow, to attain to the resurrection from the dead.

PHILIPPIANS 3:10–11 NIV

We are transfigured much like the Messiah, our lives gradually becoming brighter and more beautiful as God enters our lives and we become like him.

2 CORINTHIANS 3:18 THE MESSAGE

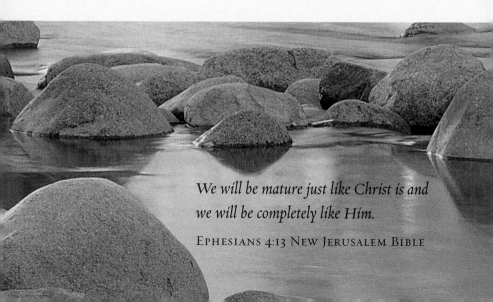

We will be mature just like Christ is and we will be completely like Him.

EPHESIANS 4:13 NEW JERUSALEM BIBLE

Discipleship—the process of becoming like Christ—al
begins with a decision.

> *"Come, be my disciple," Jesus said to him. So Matthew got up and*
> *followed him.*
>
> MATTHEW 9:9 NLT

Once you decide to get serious about becoming like Christ, you must
begin to act in new ways. You can be certain that the Holy Spirit will
help you with these changes.

> *Continue to work out your salvation with fear and trembling, for it is God*
> *who works in you to will and to act according to his good purpose.*
>
> PHILIPPIANS 2:12–13 NIV

The "work out" is your responsibility, and the "work in" is God's role.

Your first step in spiritual growth is to start changing the way you *think*. The way you think determines the way you *feel*, and the way you feel influences the way you *act*.

*Be careful how you think; your life
is shaped by your thoughts.*

PROVERBS 4:23 TEV

Let God transform you into a new person by changing the way you think.

ROMANS 12:2 NLT

*There must be a spiritual renewal
of your thoughts and attitudes.*

EPHESIANS 4:23 NLT

*Stop thinking like children. In regard to evil be infants,
but in your thinking be adults.*

1 CORINTHIANS 14:20 NIV

Those who live following their sinful selves think only about things that their sinful selves want. But those who live following the Spirit are thinking about the things the Spirit wants them to do.

When I was a child, I talked like a child, I thought like a child, I reasoned like a child. When I became a man, I put childish ways behind me.

God has given us his Spirit. That's why we don't think the same way that the people of this world think.

Let God transform you inwardly by
a complete change of your mind. Then you will
be able to know the will of God—
what is good and is pleasing to him and is perfect.

ROMANS 12:2 TEV

An important thing to remember is that God is *not* in a hurry to make you a disciple. In fact, he will take your entire lifetime to mold you and make you like Christ. *We* get in a hurry but *he* isn't in a hurry.

Often we get discouraged and think, "I'm not growing. I'm not going fast enough." But God has promised to never give up on us. The Bible has promised:

God who began a good work in us
will bring it to the day of completion.

PHILIPPIANS 1:6 NEW JERUSALEM BIBLE

Everything on earth has its own time and its own season.

ECCLESIASTES 3:1 CEV

You have begun to live the new life,
in which you are being made new and are
becoming like the One who made you.

COLOSSIANS 3:10 NCV

Spiritual maturity is neither instant nor automatic; it is a gradual, progressive development that will take the rest of your life. Becoming like Christ is a long, slow process of growth.

We can't even imagine what we will be like when Christ returns. But we do know that when he comes we will be like him, for we will see him as he really is.

1 JOHN 3:2 NLT

Don't become so well-adjusted to your culture that you fit into it without even thinking. Instead, fix your attention on God. You'll be changed from the inside out. ... Unlike the culture around you, always dragging you down to its level of immaturity, God brings the best out of you, develops well-formed maturity in you.

ROMANS 12:2 THE MESSAGE

lthough God could instantly transform us, he has chosen to develop us slowly. Why does it take so long to change and grow up?

We are slow learners.

You were taught, with regard to your former way of life,
to put off your old self, which is being corrupted by its deceitful desires;
to be made new in the attitude of your minds.

Ephesians 4:22–23 NIV

We have a lot to unlearn.

Now you must rid yourselves of all such things as these: anger, rage, malice,
slander, and filthy language from your lips. Do not lie to each other,
since you have taken off your old self with its practices and have put on the
new self, which is being renewed in knowledge in the image of its Creator.

Colossians 3:8–10 NIV

Habits take time to develop.

Practice [spiritual disciplines]. Devote your life to them so that everyone
can see your progress.

1 Timothy 4:15 GWT

Y ou were created to be like Christ—the third purpose of your life is to grow in Discipleship. This is the very reason that your heart beats. This is the very reason for each breath you take.

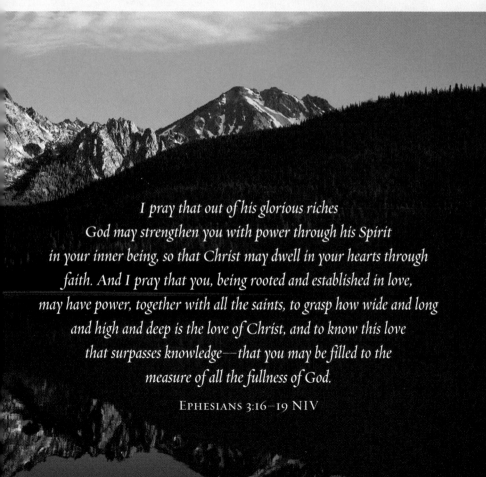

I pray that out of his glorious riches
God may strengthen you with power through his Spirit
in your inner being, so that Christ may dwell in your hearts through
faith. And I pray that you, being rooted and established in love,
may have power, together with all the saints, to grasp how wide and long
and high and deep is the love of Christ, and to know this love
that surpasses knowledge—that you may be filled to the
measure of all the fullness of God.

EPHESIANS 3:16–19 NIV

You Were Shaped for Serving God!

God has made us what we are.
And in Christ Jesus, God has made us to
do good works which God planned in
advance for us to live our lives doing.

Ephesians 2:10 NCV

Whenever God gives us an assignment, he always equips us with what we need to accomplish it. This custom combination of capabilities is called your SHAPE.

You shaped me first inside, then out; you formed me in my mother's womb.

PSALM 139:13 THE MESSAGE

S.H.A.P.E. stands for:

S—Spiritual Gifts: Special gifts given by the Holy Spirit so you can help build up the church.

H—Heart: Special passions, things that you feel strongly about, to drive you to service.

A—Abilities: Natural talents built into you from birth.

P—Personality: Your uniqueness, what makes you different from every one else.

E—Experiences: Situations and circumstances you face that help you empathize with others.

God has wired you up with these five things to make you you.

*Y*our hands shaped me and made me, LORD.

JOB 10:8 NIV

You made all the delicate, inner parts of my body
and knit me together in my mother's womb.
Thank you for making me so wonderfully complex!
Your workmanship is marvelous, LORD.

PSALM 139:13–14 NLT

Every day of my life was recorded in your book, LORD.
Every moment was laid out before a single day had passed.

PSALM 139:16 NLT

SPIRITUAL GIFTS: These are God-empowered abilities for serving him that are given only to believers.

We have different gifts, according to the grace given us. If a man's gift is prophesying, let him use it in proportion to his faith. If it is serving, let him serve; if it is teaching, let him teach; if it is encouraging, let him encourage; if it is contributing to the needs of others, let him give generously; if it is leadership, let him govern diligently; if it is showing mercy, let him do it cheerfully.

ROMANS 12:6–8 NIV

It was God who gave some to be apostles, some to be prophets, some to be evangelists, and some to be pastors and teachers, to prepare God's people for works of service, so that the body of Christ may be built up.

EPHESIANS 4:11–12 NIV

Each man has his own gift from God; one has this gift, another has that.

1 CORINTHIANS 7:7 NIV

Christ has generously divided out his gifts to us.

EPHESIANS 4:7 CEV

It is the one and only Holy Spirit who distributes these gifts. He alone decides which gift each person should have.

1 CORINTHIANS 12:11 NLT

A spiritual gift is given to each of us as a means of helping the entire church.

1 CORINTHIANS 12:7 NLT

There are different kinds of service in the church, but it is the same Lord we are serving.

1 CORINTHIANS 12:5 NLT

HEART: Your heart represents the source of all your motivations—what you love to do and what you care about most. Another word for heart is passion. Don't ignore your interests. Consider how they might be used for God's glory. There is a reason that you love to do these things.

As a face is reflected in water, so the heart reflects the person.

PROVERBS 27:19 NLT

Serve the LORD with all your heart.

1 SAMUEL 12:20 NIV

Above all else, guard your heart,
for it is the wellspring of life.

PROVERBS 4:23 NIV

ABILITIES: Your abilities are the natural talents you were born with.

All our abilities come from God. God has given each of us the ability to do certain things well.

Romans 12:6 NLT

There are different abilities to perform service, but the same God gives ability to all for their particular service.

1 Corinthians 12:6 TEV

Remember the LORD your God, for it is he who gives you the ability to produce wealth.

Deuteronomy 8:18 NIV

What I'm *able* to do, God *wants* me to do. No one else can play your role, because they don't have the unique shape that God has given you.

God has given each of you some special abilities;

be sure to use them to help each other,

passing on to others God's many kinds of blessings.

1 PETER 4:10 LB

PERSONALITY: God created each of us with a unique combination of personality traits. There is no "right" or "wrong" temperament for ministry. We need all kinds of personalities to balance the church and give it flavor.

God works through different people

in different ways, but it is the same God who

achieves his purpose through them all.

1 CORINTHIANS 12:6 Ph

EXPERIENCES are one of the most important things that God uses to shape you for service. There are five kinds of experiences God uses:

- *Family experiences*—interactions with parents, children, spouses and anyone you call family.

- *Vocational experiences*—everything you learn on the job, from skills to getting along with others.

- *Educational experiences*—times of learning throughout your life, from elementary school to continuing discovery as an adult.

- *Spiritual experiences*—those special moments of incredible closeness with God, when you discover something new about who he is and who you are in him.

But most important of all:

- *Painful experiences*—disappointments, hurts, and sorrows that cause you to lean heavily on God, and that develop empathy in your heart for the hurts of others.

Painful experiences are hard to understand. We ask God, "Why me?"

But ...

- Who can better help someone with cancer than someone who has battled cancer themselves?

- Who can better help somebody going through the pain of their parents' divorce than somebody else who has gone through the same thing?

- Who can better help a student with a learning disability than somebody who has also struggled with learning difficulties?

Often, the very thing that you struggle most with in your life, the very thing you like the least, the very thing you're most embarrassed and ashamed of, is the very thing God wants to use to help you minister to others. God uses not just our strengths. He also uses our weaknesses.

Jesus said, "My grace is sufficient for you, for my power is made perfect in weakness." Therefore I will boast all the more gladly about my weaknesses, so that Christ's power may rest on me.

2 CORINTHIANS 12:9 NIV

hy does God use our weaknesses? Because when he does, he gets all the glory. If somebody does something great using their own obvious strengths, people see it and say, "Well, he's just good at that. Of course it will be a success." But if somebody does something wonderful in an area that is obviously not their strength, people say, "Wow! Maybe there's hope for me! If God can do that for them, he can surely do that for me!"

For Christ's sake, I delight in weaknesses,

in insults, in hardships, in persecutions, in difficulties.

For when I am weak, then I am strong.

2 CORINTHIANS 12:10 NIV

God is giving you a special S.H.A.P.E. Using your special abilities, gifts, and life experiences for the benefit of others is called *Ministry*—the fourth purpose of your life.

God has given each of you some special abilities. Be sure to use them to help each other, passing on to others God's many kinds of blessing.

1 Corinthians 12:7 New Jerusalem Bible

No matter who you are, if you allow God to shape your life, you can be used by him for great things. There is one key qualification, though:

Those who make themselves clean from all ... evil things, will be used for special purposes, because they are dedicated and useful to their Master, ready to be used for every good deed.

2 Timothy 2:21 TEV

God can use small vessels. God can use plain vessels. God can even use broken vessels. But he will not use a dirty vessel. You've got to be clean.

The good news is you can be clean simply by asking.

If we confess our sins, God is faithful and just and will forgive us our sins and purify us from all unrighteousness.

1 John 1:9 NIV

To discover your shape, begin by assessing your gifts and abilities.

Don't act thoughtlessly, but try to find out and do whatever the Lord wants you to.

EPHESIANS 5:17 LB

Try to have a sane estimate of your capabilities.

ROMANS 12:3 PH.

Consider your heart and your personality.

Make a careful exploration of who you are and the work you have been given, and then sink yourself into that.

GALATIANS 6:4 THE MESSAGE

Examine your experiences and extract the lessons you have learned.

Remember today what you have learned about the Lord *through your experiences with him.*

Deuteronomy 11:2 TEV

Since God knows what's best for you, you should gratefully accept the way he fashioned you.

What right have you, a human being, to cross-examine God? The pot has no right to say to the potter: "Why did you make me this shape?" Surely a potter can do what he likes with the clay!

Romans 9:20–21 New Jerusalem Bible

Christ has given each of us special abilities—whatever he wants us to have out of his rich storehouse of gifts.

Ephesians 4:7 LB

Part of accepting your shape is recognizing your limitations. God assigns each of us a field or sphere of service.

Our goal is to stay within the boundaries of God's plan for us.

2 CORINTHIANS 10:13 NLT

Let us run with patience the particular race that God has set before us.

HEBREWS 12:1 LB

Be sure to do what you should, for then you will enjoy the personal satisfaction of having done your work well, and you won't need to compare yourself to anyone else.

GALATIANS 6:4 NLT

We do not dare to classify or compare ourselves with some who commend themselves. When they measure themselves by themselves and compare themselves with themselves, they are not wise.

2 CORINTHIANS 10:12 NIV

Keep developing your shape. We are to cultivate our gifts and abilities, keep our hearts aflame, grow our character and personality, and broaden our experiences so we will be increasingly more effective in our service. Do you like kids? Volunteer at an after-school club or to teach Sunday school. Can you sing? Join the choir or sing a solo in church. Do your interests lie in the area of business and finance? Find out if the finance committee at church has an opening. God has given you some great gifts to use for him.

Keep on growing in your knowledge and understanding.

PHILIPPIANS 1:9 NLT

Kindle afresh the gift of God which is in you.

2 TIMOTHY 1:6 NASB

Be sure to use the abilities God has given you. ... Put these abilities to work.

1 TIMOTHY 4:14–15 LB

Concentrate on doing your best for God, work you won't be ashamed of.

2 TIMOTHY 2:15 THE MESSAGE

Like athletes preparing for the Olympics, we keep training for that big day.

They do it for a gold medal that tarnishes and fades.
You're after one that's gold eternally.

1 CORINTHIANS 9:25 THE MESSAGE

We serve God by serving others. How can you have the heart of a servant?

Real servants make themselves available to serve.

No soldier in active service entangles himself in the affairs of everyday life, so that he may please the one who enlisted him.

2 Timothy 2:4 NASB

Being a servant means giving up the right to control your schedule and allowing God to interrupt it whenever he needs to.

Real servants pay attention to needs.

Whenever we have the opportunity, we have to do what is good for everyone, especially for the family of believers.

Galatians 6:10 GWT

Never tell your neighbors to wait until tomorrow if you can help them now.

Proverbs 3:28 TEV

Real servants do every task with equal dedication.

Jesus said, "You call me 'Teacher' and 'Lord,' and rightly so, for that is what I am. Now that I, your Lord and Teacher, have washed your feet, you also should wash one another's feet. I have set you an example that you should do as I have done for you. I tell you the truth, no servant is greater than his master, nor is a messenger greater than the one who sent him. Now that you know these things, you will be blessed if you do them."

JOHN 13:13–17 NIV

"Whoever can be trusted with very little can also be trusted with much."

LUKE 16:10 NIV

Real servants maintain a low profile.

Jesus said, "When you do good deeds, don't try to show off. If you do, you won't get a reward from your Father in heaven."

MATTHEW 6:1 CEV

When Christ ... shows up again on this earth, you'll show up, too— the real you, the glorious you. Meanwhile, be content with obscurity.

COLOSSIANS 3:4 THE MESSAGE

God's Power in Your Weakness

 e are weak ... yet by God's power we will live with him to serve you.

2 Corinthians 13:4 NIV

Jesus said, "I am with you; that is all you need. My power shows up best in weak people."

2 Corinthians 12:9 LB

God loves to use weak people. Usually we deny our weaknesses, defend them, excuse them, hide them, and resent them. This prevents God from using them the way he desires. God has a different perspective on your weaknesses.

"My thoughts and my ways are higher than yours," says the LORD.

ISAIAH 55:9 CEV

God purposely chose ... what the world considers weak in order to shame the powerful.

1 Corinthians 1:27 TEV

We are like clay jars in which this treasure [of the gospel] is stored. The real power comes from God and not from us.

2 Corinthians 4:7 CEV

he fourth purpose for your life is ministry—serving others through serving God.

You were made to minister, so when you start to get run down you can pray:

"God, light that fire again in my heart. I was planned for your pleasure, so help me to worship you. I was formed for your family, so let me fellowship. I was created to be like Christ, so keep me growing. I was shaped to serve you, so help me to be faithful in my ministry."

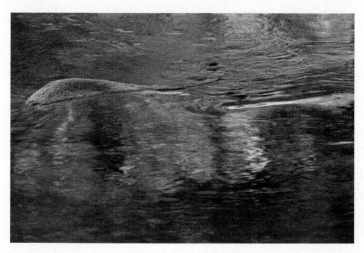

The one who calls you is faithful and he will do it.

1 Thessalonians 5:24 NIV

YOU WERE MADE
FOR A MISSION!

Jesus prayed, "In the same way that you [God] gave me
a mission in the world,

I give them [my followers] a mission in the world."

JOHN 17:18 THE MESSAGE

G od has given us a mission in life.

Through Christ, God has made peace between us and Himself and
He gave us the work of telling everyone the peace we can have with Him.
So we have been sent to speak for Christ.

2 Corinthians 5:19–20 New Jerusalem Bible

If you want God's blessing and power on your life, you must care about what God cares about most, and the biggest concern of God's heart is bringing his lost children back home to him.

The fruit of the righteous is a tree of life,
and he who wins souls is wise.

Proverbs 11:30 NIV

God ... through Christ changed us
from enemies into his friends and gave us the
task of making others his friends also.

2 Corinthians 5:18 TEV

The Importance of Your Mission

Fulfilling your life mission on earth is an essential part of living for God's glory. The Bible gives several reasons why your mission is so important.

1. Your mission is a continuation of Jesus' mission on earth. As his followers, we are to continue what Jesus started.

> *Jesus said, "Go to the people of all nations and make them my disciples. Baptize them in the name of the Father, the Son, and the Holy Spirit, and teach them to do everything I have told you."*
>
> Matthew 28:19–20 CEV

"You must warn [unbelievers] so they may live. If you don't speak out to warn the wicked to stop their evil ways, they will die in their sin," says the Lord.

Ezekiel 3:18 NCV

You are the only Christian some people will ever know, and your mission is to share Jesus with them.

2. Your mission is a wonderful privilege. Although it is a big responsibility, it is also an incredible honor to be used by God.

God has given us the privilege of urging everyone to come into his favor and be reconciled to him.

2 CORINTHIANS 5:18 LB

We are workers together with God.

2 CORINTHIANS 6:1 NCV

We're Christ's representatives. God uses us to persuade men and women to drop their differences and enter into God's work of making things right between them. We're speaking for Christ himself now: Become friends with God.

2 CORINTHIANS 5:20 THE MESSAGE

3. **Telling others how they can have eternal life is** the greatest thing you can do for them. Everybody needs Jesus.

> *Jesus is the only One who can save people.*
>
> ACTS 4:12 NCV

4. *Your mission has eternal significance.* It will impact the eternal destiny of other people, so it's more important than any job, achievement, or goal you will reach during your life on earth.

> *Jesus said, "All of us must quickly carry out the tasks assigned us by the one who sent me, because there is little time left before the night falls and all work comes to an end."*
>
> JOHN 9:4 NLT

5. Your mission gives your life meaning.

My life is worth nothing unless I use it for doing the work assigned me by the Lord Jesus—the work of telling others the Good News about God's wonderful kindness and love.

ACTS 20:24 NLT

6. God's timetable for history's conclusion is connected to the completion of our commission. Jesus will not return until everyone God wants to hear the Good News has heard it.

Jesus said, "No one knows about that day or hour [of my return], not even the angels in heaven, nor the Son, but only the Father."

MATTHEW 24:36 NIV

Jesus said, "It is not for you to know the times or dates the Father has set by his own authority. But you will receive power when the Holy Spirit comes on you; and you will be my witnesses in Jerusalem, and in all Judea and Samaria, and to the ends of the earth."

ACTS 1:7–8 NIV

Jesus said, "The Good News about God's kingdom will be preached in all the world, to every nation. Then the end will come."

MATTHEW 24:14 NCV

Our mission on earth is to be ambassadors for God! God loves us so much that he has sent us to represent him to people who don't know him. That is your mission to the world.

The most important thing is that I complete my mission, the work that the Lord Jesus gave me— to tell people the Good News about God's grace.

ACTS 20:24 NCV

Jesus said, "As the Father has sent me, I am sending you."

JOHN 20:21 NIV

We have been sent to speak for Christ.

2 CORINTHIANS 5:20 NCV

Fulfilling your mission in the world is called *Evangelism*— the fifth purpose of your life.

Once you become part of God's family, it's your mission to tell others so they can join you, for God doesn't want anyone to be outside of his family.

Through Christ, all the kindness of God has been poured out upon us undeserving sinners; and now he is sending us out around the world to tell all people everywhere the great thing God has done for them, so they, too, will believe and obey him.

Romans 1:5 LB

The Lord is not slow in keeping his promise, as some understand slowness. He is patient with you, not wanting anyone to perish, but everyone to come to repentance.

2 Peter 3:9 NIV

"God so loved the world that he gave his one and only Son, that whoever believes in him shall not perish but have eternal life."

John 3:16 NIV

ONE MORE

My dad was a man on a mission. He was a pastor for 50 years. He was also a carpenter. He volunteered his time to build over 150 church buildings around the world, on every continent. He would take disaster teams to South America, the North Pole, Iraq, Jerusalem—all around the world. Even in his seventies he was up on rooftops, building churches in Siberia.

A few years ago, my dad died of cancer. The last week of his life, he was in a dream-like state, and he talked constantly, and in that last week, I listened to my dad dream aloud. You can learn a lot about a person by listening to their dreams. He didn't talk about the movies he'd gone to or the books he'd read. He didn't talk about his escapades in the South Pacific during World War II. He didn't talk about fishing, which he dearly loved. He talked about the deepest passion of his heart—building churches.

As he dreamed he would say aloud: "You take those two-by-fours over to that corner and make sure that joist is correct. Don't get electrocuted! Make sure they get back for lunch."

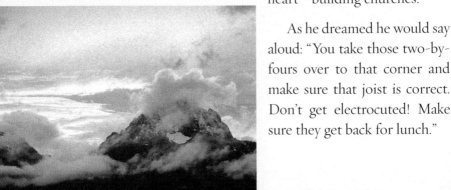

One evening, just before he died, when he was at his weakest state, my dad became very agitated, and he tried to get out of bed. My wife tried to comfort him: "No, Jimmy, you've got to lay down. You're very weak. You need to lay down."

Still, he continued to struggle to get out of bed. She said, "Jimmy, what do you want?"

He said, "Got to save one more for Jesus. Got to save one more for Jesus."

Over and over, for the next hour, he repeated this phrase. "Got to save one more for Jesus! Save one more for Jesus! Save one more for Jesus!"

I put my head down on the side of his bed and tears were coming down my face. He reached up and put his hands on my head, and he said, "Save one more for Jesus! Save one more for Jesus."

I intend for that phrase to be the theme of the rest of my life. I invite you to make it the theme for your life, too. As you consider what you will do for the rest of your life, I can assure you there is nothing more important than bringing people to Jesus.

This is our mission—bringing people to Christ so they can be built up to maturity, be trained for a ministry, be equipped for their life mission and live a life for the glory of God.

I challenge you—reach one more for Jesus.

SHARING YOUR LIFE MESSAGE

Those who believe in the Son of God have the testimony of God in them.

1 JOHN 5:10 GWT

God has given you a Life Message to share. God wants to speak to the world through you.

Your lives are echoing the Master's Word ... The news of your faith in God is out. We don't even have to say anything anymore—you're the message!

1 THESSALONIANS 1:8 THE MESSAGE

In Christ we speak the truth before God, as messengers of God.

2 CORINTHIANS 2:17 NCV

Your Life Message includes your *testimony*—the story of how Christ has made a difference in your life.

You are the ones chosen by God, chosen for the high calling of priestly work, chosen to be a holy people, God's instruments to do his work and speak out for him, to tell others of the night-and-day difference he made for you— from nothing to something, from rejected to accepted.

1 PETER 2:9–10 THE MESSAGE

Be ready at all times to answer anyone who asks you to explain the hope you have in you, but do it with gentleness and respect.

1 PETER 3:15–16 TEV

The best way to "be ready" is to write out your testimony and then memorize the main points. Divide it into four parts:

1. What my life was like before I met Jesus

2. How I realized I needed Jesus

3. How I committed my life to Jesus

4. The difference Jesus has made in my life

our Life Message includes your life lessons—the truths that God has taught you from experiences with him.

> *God, teach me lessons for living*
> *so I can stay the course.*

PSALM 119:33 THE MESSAGE

> *A warning given by an experienced person to someone willing to listen is more valuable than ... jewelry made of the finest gold.*

PROVERBS 25:12 TEV

Mature people develop the habit of extracting lessons from everyday experiences. Make a list of your life lessons. Here are a few questions to get you started:

What has God taught me ...

- from failure?
- from a lack of money?
- from pain or sorrow or depression?
- through waiting?
- from disappointment?
- from my family, my church, my relationships, my small group, and my critics?

Your Life Message includes sharing your godly passions— as you grow closer to God, he will give you a passion for something he cares about deeply so you can be a spokesman for him in the world.

Jesus said, "A man's heart determines his speech."

MATTHEW 12:34 LB

My zeal for God and his work burns hot within me.

PSALM 69:9 LB

Your message burns in my heart and bones,
    and I cannot keep silent, LORD.

JEREMIAH 20:9 CEV

It is fine to be zealous, provided the purpose is good.

GALATIANS 4:18 NIV

God gives us different passions so that everything he wants done in the world will get done.

Your Life Message includes the Good News—that when we trust God's grace to save us through what Jesus did, our sins are forgiven, we get a purpose for living, and we are promised a future home in heaven.

The Good News shows how God makes
people right with himself—that it begins and ends with faith.

Romans 1:17 NCV

God was in Christ, reconciling the world to himself,
no longer counting people's sins against them. This is
the wonderful message he has given us to tell others.

2 Corinthians 5:19 NLT

Christ's love compels us, because we are convinced that one died for all.

2 Corinthians 5:14 NIV

God has never made a person he didn't love. Everybody matters to him. When Jesus stretched out his arms wide on the cross, he was saying, "I love you this much!" Whenever you feel apathetic about your mission in the world, spend some time thinking about what Jesus did for you on the cross.

If you've been afraid to share the Good News with those around you, ask God to fill your heart with his love for them.

There is no fear in love; perfect love drives out all fear.

1 JOHN 4:18 TEV

God does not want anyone to be lost, but he wants all people to change their hearts and lives.

2 PETER 3:9 NCV

Make the most of your chances to tell others the Good News. Be wise in all your contacts with them.

COLOSSIANS 4:5 LB

Is anyone going to be in heaven because of you? Imagine the joy of greeting people in heaven whom you helped get there.

Y ou have a choice to make. You will either be a *world-class* Christian or a *worldly* Christian. Worldly Christians look to God primarily for personal fulfillment. They are saved, but self-centered. It's a "me-first" faith: How can God make *my* life more comfortable? They want to use God for their purposes instead of *being* used for *his* purposes.

In contrast, world-class Christians know they were saved to serve and made for a mission. They are eager to receive a personal assignment and excited about the privilege of being used by God. World-class Christians are the only *fully alive* people on the planet. Their joy, confidence, and enthusiasm are contagious because they know they're making a difference.

What type of Christian do you want to be?

How to Think Like
a World-Class Christian

1. *Shift from self-centered thinking* to other-centered thinking.

My friends, stop thinking like children. Think like mature people.

1 Corinthians 14:20 CEV

This is the first step to becoming a world-class Christian. Children only think of themselves; grown-ups think of others.

Don't think only about your own affairs, but be interested in others, too.

Philippians 2:4 NLT

The only way we can make this switch is by a moment-by-moment dependence on God. Fortunately he doesn't leave us to struggle on our own.

God has given us his Spirit. That's why we don't think the same way that the people of this world think.

1 Corinthians 2:12 CEV

Your goal is to figure out where others are in their spiritual journey and then do whatever will bring them a step closer to knowing Christ.

I don't think about what would be good for me but about what would be good for many people so that they might be saved.

1 Corinthians 10:33 GWT

2. Shift from local thinking to global thinking.

God is a global God. He has always cared about the entire world.

From one person God made all nations who live on earth, and he decided when and where every nation would be. God has done all this, so that we will look for him and reach out and find him.

ACTS 17:26–27 CEV

The first way to start thinking globally is to begin praying for specific countries. World-class Christians pray for the world. Get a globe or a map and pray for nations by name.

"If you ask me, I will give you the nations;
     all the people on earth will be yours," says the Lord.

PSALM 2:8 NCV

What should you pray for? The Bible tells us to pray for opportunities to witness, for courage to speak up, for those who will believe, for the rapid spread of the message, and for more workers.

The best way to switch to global thinking is to just get up and go on a short-term mission project to another country! There's simply no substitute for hands-on, real life experience in another culture.

Jesus said, "You will tell everyone about me in Jerusalem, in all Judea, in Samaria, and everywhere in the world."

ACTS 1:8 CEV

3. Shift from "here and now" thinking to eternal thinking.

To make the most of your time on earth, you must maintain an eternal perspective. This will keep you from majoring on minor issues and help you distinguish between what's urgent and what's ultimate.

> *We fix our eyes not on what is seen, but on what is unseen. For what is seen is temporary, but what is unseen is eternal.*
>
> 2 Corinthians 4:18 NIV

> *Deal as sparingly as possible with the things the world thrusts on you. This world as you see it is on its way out.*
>
> 1 Corinthians 7:31 The Message

What's keeping you from being a world-class Christian? Whatever it is, let it go.

> *Let us strip off anything that slows us down or holds us back.*
>
> Hebrews 21:1 LB

You've probably heard the expression "You can't take it with you"—but the Bible says you can send it on ahead by investing in people who are going there!

> *By doing this they will be storing up real treasure for themselves in heaven—it is the only safe investment for eternity! And they will be living a fruitful Christian life down here as well.*
>
> 1 Timothy 6:19 LB

4. *Shift from thinking of excuses* to thinking of creative ways to fulfill your commission.

Whether it was Sarah claiming she was too old to be used by God or Jeremiah claiming he was too young, God rejected their excuses.

"Don't say that," the LORD replied, "for you must go wherever I send you and say whatever I tell you. And don't be afraid of the people, for I will be with you and take care of you."

JEREMIAH 1:7–8 NLT

Maybe you have believed that you needed a special "call" from God, and you've been waiting for some supernatural feeling or experience. But God has already stated his call repeatedly. We are all called to fulfill God's five purposes for our lives: to worship, to fellowship, to grow like Christ, to serve, and to be on a mission with God in the world. God doesn't want to use just *some* of his people; he wants to use *all* of his people.

There are over 6 billion people on earth, and Jesus wants all his lost children found.

Jesus said, "Only those who throw away their lives for my sake and for the sake of the Good News will ever know what it means to really live!"

MARK 8:35 LB

BALANCING YOUR LIFE

Blessed are the balanced; they shall outlast everyone. Your life is a pentathlon of five purposes, which you must keep in balance. Keeping these five purposes in balance is not easy. We all tend to overemphasize the purposes we feel most passionate about and neglect the others. If you are serious about staying on track, you will need to develop four important habits.

1. Talk through your spiritual life and its progress with a spiritual partner or small group.

As iron sharpens iron,

   so people can improve each other.

PROVERBS 27:17 NCV

We learn best in community. Our minds are sharpened and our convictions are deepened through conversation. Remember, we are meant to grow together, not separately.

Encourage each other and give each other strength.

1 THESSALONIANS 5:11 NCV

2. *Give yourself a regular spiritual check-up.*

God places a high value on the habit of self-evaluation. At least five times in Scripture we are told to test and examine our own spiritual health.

> *Test yourselves to make sure you are solid in the faith. Don't drift along taking everything for granted. Give yourselves regular checkups...test it out. If you fail the test, do something about it.*
>
> 2 CORINTHIANS 13:5 THE MESSAGE

Let's take a good look at the way we're living and reorder our lives under God.

LAMENTATIONS 3:40 THE MESSAGE

For your spiritual health you need to regularly check the five vital signs of worship, fellowship, growth in character, ministry, and mission. You can use the "Purpose Driven Health Assessment" on the next three pages to help you do your own spiritual health checkup.

Purpose Driven Health Assessment

(Rate each statement with a number, 1-5. A 1 means "I'm just beginning on this," 3 means "I'm getting going," and 5 means "I am well developed in this area.")

WORSHIP: *You were planned for God's pleasure.*

____I am experiencing more of the presence and power of God in my everyday life.

____I am faithfully attending my small group and weekend services to worship God.

____I am seeking to please God by surrendering to him every area of my life (health, decisions, finances, relationships, future, etc.)

____I am accepting the things I cannot change and becoming more grateful for the life God has given me.

FELLOWSHIP: *You were formed for God's family.*

____I am deepening my understanding of and friendship with God in community with others.

____I am growing in my ability both to share and to show my love to others.

____I am willing to share my real needs for prayer and support from others.

_____I am resolving conflict constructively and am willing to forgive others.

DISCIPLESHIP: *You were created to become like Christ.*

_____I have a growing relationship with God through regular time in the Bible and in prayer (spiritual habits).

_____I am experiencing more of the characteristics of Jesus Christ (love, joy, peace, patience, kindness, self-control, etc.) in my life.

_____I am avoiding addictive behaviors (too much food, television, busyness, and the like) to meet my needs.

_____I am spending time with a Christian friend (spiritual partner) who celebrates and challenges my spiritual growth.

MINISTRY: *You were shaped for serving God.*

_____I have discovered and am further developing my unique God-given shape for ministry.

_____I am regularly asking God to show me opportunities to serve him and others.

_____I am serving in a regular (once a month or more) ministry in the church or community.

_____I am a team player in my small group by sharing some group role or responsibility.

EVANGELISM: *You were made for a mission.*

_____I am cultivating relationships with non-Christians and asking God to give me opportunities to share his love.

_____I am investing my time in another person or group who needs to know Christ personally.

_____I am regularly inviting unchurched or unconnected friends to my church or small group.

_____I am praying and learning about where God can use me and our group cross-culturally for missions.

Total your answers in each individual section and use this guide to evaluate how you're doing and where you need to improve:

Just Beginning 0-5

Fair 5-10

Getting Going 10-15

Very Good 15-20

Well Developed 20-25

My prayer for you is this:

When your life is through people will say,

"He served God. She reached people for Jesus."

This mission isn't easy, but don't give up.

The rewards are beyond anything you could imagine.

Evangelism—bringing people to Jesus—

is the fifth purpose for your life.

David ... *served the purpose of God in his own generation.*

Acts 13:36 NASB

This phrase is the ultimate definition of a life well lived. You do the eternal and timeless (God's purpose) in a contemporary and timely way (in your generation). That is what the *purpose-driven life* is all about. Neither past nor future generations can serve God's purpose in this generation. Only we can. Will you be a person God can use for his purposes? Will you serve God's purpose in your generation?

When fulfilling your purposes seems tough, don't give in to discouragement. Remember your reward, which will last forever.

> *No eye has seen,*
> *   no ear has heard,*
> *no mind has conceived*
> *   what God has prepared for those who love him.*

1 Corinthians 2:9 NIV

> *I consider that our present sufferings are not worth comparing with the glory that will be revealed in us.*

Romans 8:18 NIV

> *Jesus says, "Behold, I am coming soon! My reward is with me, and I will give to everyone according to what he has done."*

Revelation 22:12 NIV

A Prayer for Your Purpose

Father, more than anything else I want to live for you and the five purposes that you created me to fulfill.

I want my life to bring you pleasure as I live a lifestyle of worship.

I want to be used to build the fellowship of your family, the church.

I want to become like Jesus in the way I think and feel and act.

I want to use the shape you've given me for a ministry to other believers in the Body of Christ.

I want to fulfill my mission in the world by telling others about your love. Help me to reach one more for Jesus. Help me to pass on the message of your purposes to others.

Dear Lord, I want to serve your purposes in my generation, so that one day I may hear you say, "Well done, good and faithful servant."

In Jesus' name, Amen.

You were made to live a purpose-driven life!

1. **WORSHIP:** You were planned for God's pleasure!

   Worship the LORD with gladness;
   come before him with joyful songs.

   PSALM 100:2 NIV

2. **FELLOWSHIP:** You were formed for a family!

   "I will be a Father to you,
   and you will be my sons and daughters,"
   says the Lord Almighty.

   2 CORINTHIANS 6:18 NIV

3. **DISCIPLESHIP:** You were created to become like Christ!

   If we are children, then we are heirs—heirs of God and co-heirs with Christ, if indeed
   we share in his sufferings in order that we may also share in his glory.

   ROMANS 8:17 NIV

4. **MINISTRY:** You were shaped for serving God!

   This service that you perform is not only supplying the needs of God's people but is
   also overflowing in many expressions of thanks to God.

   2 CORINTHIANS 9:12 NIV

5. **EVANGELISM:** You were made for a mission!

   Jesus said, "Go and make disciples of all nations, baptizing them in the name of the
   Father and of the Son and of the Holy Spirit, and teaching them to obey everything I
   have commanded you. And surely I am with you always, to the very end of the age."

   MATTHEW 28:19–20 NIV

Sources

Text compiled from: A sermon entitled "What on Earth Am I Here For?" by Pastor Rick Warren of Saddleback Church

The Purpose-Driven Life. By Rick Warren. © 2002 by Rick Warren. Grand Rapids, MI: Zondervan, 2002.

Scripture marked NASB was taken from the NEW AMERICAN STANDARD BIBLE ®, copyright © 1960, 1962, 1963, 1968, 1971, 1972, 1973, 1975, 1977, 1995 by The Lockman Foundation. Used by permission.

Scripture marked NLT was taken from the *Holy Bible, New Living Translation,* copyright © 1996. Used by permission of Tyndale House Publishers, Inc., Wheaton, Illinois 60189. All rights reserved.

Scripture marked TEV was taken from the *Good News Bible in Today's English Version*— Second Edition, copyright © 1992 by American Bible Society. Used by permission.

Scripture marked LB was taken from the *Holy Bible, The Living Translation,* copyright © 1988. Used by permission of Tyndale House Publishers, Inc., Wheaton, Illinois 60189. All rights reserved.

Scripture marked NCV was quoted from *The Holy Bible, New Century Version,* copyright © 1987, 1988, 1991 by Word Publishing, Dallas, Texas 75039. Used by permission.

Scripture marked THE MESSAGE was taken from *The Message.* Copyright © by Eugene H. Peterson, 1993, 1994, 1995. Used by permission of NavPress Publishing Group.

Scripture marked NEW JERUSALEM BIBLE was taken from *The New Jerusalem Bible.* Copyright © Doubleday & Company, Inc., 1985, New York. Used by permission.

Scripture marked PH is taken from the *New Testament in Modern English* by J. B. Phillips, copyright © 1958 by Macmillan, New York, NY. Used by permission.

Scripture marked CEV is taken from the *Contemporary English Version,* copyright © 1995 by the American Bible Society, New York, NY. Used by permission.

Scripture marked GWT is taken from *God's Word Translation,* copyright © 1995 by World Publishing, Inc., Grand Rapids, MI. Used by permission.

Scripture marked NRSV is taken from the *New Revised Standard Version,* copyright © 1990 by Zondervan, Grand Rapids, MI. Used by permission.

Scripture marked KJV was taken from the *Holy Bible, King James Version.* Public Domain.

At Inspirio we love to hear from you—
your stories, your feedback,
and your product ideas.
Please send your comments to us
by way of e-mail at
icares@zondervan.com
or to the address below:

inspirio

Attn: Inspirio Cares
5300 Patterson Avenue SE
Grand Rapids, MI 49530

If you would like further information
about Inspirio and the products we
create please visit us at:
www.inspiriogifts.com

Thank you and God Bless!